I Have a Pet!

by Shari Halpern

HOUGHTON MIFFLIN COMPANY

BOSTON

ATLANTA   DALLAS   GENEVA, ILLINOIS   PALO ALTO   PRINCETON

The author wishes to thank Damian
Salgado of Hoboken House of Reptiles for
his assistance.

1997 Impression
Houghton Mifflin Edition, 1996

For Paul
(and Fern)

I have a pet!

My dog's name is Bucky. I take him out for his walks.
He is curious and likes to sniff everything. Bucky is also
smart. I taught him to sit and to give me his paw.

I give Bucky a bath when he is dirty. It is a big job, and
sometimes Bucky doesn't cooperate. But when his bath
is done, he smells nice and clean. I love my dog.

I have a pet!

This is my cat, Fern. I help take Fern to the vet so she can get her vaccinations. They keep her healthy. Every year we make sure Fern goes for shots.

My favorite time with Fern is at night when I'm about to
go to sleep. She curls up in a little ball near my pillow,
and I can hear her purring. That means she's happy.
I love my cat.

I have a pet!

My pet is a bird, and his name is George. He is a parakeet. I give George birdseed and water, and I change the paper at the bottom of his cage when it gets dirty.

George sings. Sometimes he chirps softly, and other times he squawks loudly. Sometimes he stands on my shoulder and sings to me. I love my bird.

I have a pet!

Sophie is my hamster. I give her food and water, and I clean out her cage. I take out the old, dirty wood chips and put in new, clean ones. Sophie likes to burrow under them and make a soft bed to sleep in.

I like to hold Sophie in my hands and watch her little pink nose wiggle up and down. She is so small and her fur is so smooth. I am very gentle with her. I love my hamster.

24

I have a pet!

This is my pet lizard. His name is Raymond. He lives in a glass cage with a rock and a branch that he likes to sit on. I make sure Raymond gets fresh water and crickets to eat.

I like to hold Raymond. He doesn't feel slimy. He feels dry and smooth. Sometimes Raymond sheds his skin. I think Raymond is an interesting pet. I love my lizard.

29

Which pet would *you* like to have?